How to Raise
Test Scores

Robin Fogarty

SkyLight
Professional
Development

Arlington Heights, Illinois

How to Raise Test Scores

Published by SkyLight Professional Development
2626 S. Clearbrook Dr., Arlington Heights, IL 60005-5310
800-348-4474, 847-290-6600
Fax 847-290-6609
info@skylightedu.com
http://www.skylightedu.com

Senior Vice President, Product Development: Robin Fogarty
Director, Product Development: Ela Aktay
Senior Editor: Amy Kinsman
Editor: Jodi Keller
Proofreader: Jill Oldham
Book Designer: Donna Ramirez
Cover Designer: David Stockman
Production Supervisor: Bob Crump
Production Assistant: Christina Georgi
Researcher: Barb Lightner

Printed in the United States of America.
ISBN 1-57517-163-5

2475-McN
Item no. 1751

Z Y X W V U T S R Q P O N M L K J I H G F E D C
06 05 04 03 02 01   15 14 13 12 11 10 9 8 7 6

Contents

Introduction

In today's society there is much concern about test scores. Teachers, parents, and community leaders are concerned about how their students or children perform on state and other standardized tests. There is much speculation about what educators can do to address this concern. Often monetary grants for tutoring, literacy programs, and other educational supports are proposed as options, yet many educators, teachers, and parents agree that this concern needs to be addressed at the most basic level—as it relates to the teaching and learning process.

How to Raise Test Scores illustrates proven instructional strategies that get results. Teachers can support and prepare their students for test taking, as well as for academic and lifelong success, by incorporating the techniques outlined in this booklet. These methods help students become more familiar with, have more knowledge about, and be better prepared, not only for taking tests, but for living life. If a teacher can help students improve their communication skills, learn how to mediate their thinking strategies, and understand the best way to attack a question, positive results will be evidenced through increased test scores. These and other important techniques are outlined in the pages that follow, along with suggestions for further reading regarding each of the strategies. Teachers can implement some of these strategies immediately and others over time to see student test scores rise.

How to Raise Test Scores is developed in the structure of an acronym (see Figure 1). Every letter in the phrase "Test Scores" represents the first letter of a

TEST

 each *for* the test, not *to* the test
Approach instruction as assessment; teach for conceptual understandings and life skills (what students know and are able to do); use big ideas; and stress transfer, application, and performance through a multiple intelligences approach. (Perkins and Salomon; Gardner; Eisner; Noller; Parnes and Biondi)

 xpect the best; accept no less
Set high expectations; use grade level or developmentally appropriate materials for all; enhance skill building with enrichment and acceleration as needed; use standards and benchmarks. (TESA-Kerman; Caine and Caine; Rowe)

 tructure with cooperative learning
Use small group interactions to foster student-to-student dialogue and articulation; help students to hear what they and others are saying as they put ideas into their own words. (Johnson and Johnson; Kagan; Bellanca and Fogarty; Goleman; Joyce)

 each test-taking strategies explicitly
Demonstrate techniques for true/false, multiple choice, and essay questions; show how to outline or web ideas for quick reference and what students can do if they don't know the answers. Use metacognitive reflections to anchor learning. (Ogle; Brown)

Figure 1

SCORES

S tress prelearning strategies
Emphasize prelearning strategies that tap into prior knowledge and background experience; create fertile mindsets for learning. (Wolfe; Sylwester; Caine & Caine; Anderson et al.)

C hunk the material for deep understanding
Cluster ideas together into chunks that make sense; foster connection-making and personal understanding of information; promote transfer through patterns and meaning. (Wolfe; Sylwester)

O rganize with graphics
Utilize graphic organizers to make student thinking visible; adapt advanced organizers as ways to gather information or as methods for reviewing material. (Ausubel; Lyman & McTighe; Gardner)

R eflect through mediation
Foster reflective thinking and take time to make sense of things by mediating the learning with questions, logs, think-aloud partner dialogues, and other reflective tools. (Feuerstein; Whimbey & Lockhead)

E xpress ideas with mnemonic devices and visual cues
Teach memory devices to aid in learning; use acronyms, rhymes, and other sound-alike devices; use visualization techniques of color, action, and exaggeration as well as metaphors to trigger short-term memory and to internalize for long-term retrieval. (Lorayne; Lucas; Joyce & Showers; Wolfe; Walberg)

S eek student choices in learning situations
Allow freedom of choice within a given structure; capitalize on student interest and self-selection opportunities; create personally relevant learning; build in self-assessments and evaluation. (Sylwester; Goleman; Stepien & Gallagher; Stiggins)

Figure 1 (continued)
SkyLight Professional Development

different technique that educators can use to raise test scores. For example, the "s" in "Test" represents the method "Structure with Cooperative Learning." Teachers can then read about why structuring with cooperative learning is beneficial to test taking and how they can use it in their classroom to raise test scores. Each letter of the phrase has a strategy, providing teachers with ten different strategies to implement to increase test scores. These methods teach students how to best utilize their intelligences and cognitive and cooperative skills to accomplish classroom tasks, to improve test-taking results, and to achieve lifelong endeavors.

T Teach *for* the Test, Not *to* the Test

To help students learn, not just for the test but for a lifetime, approach instruction as assessment. For, as Eisner (1983) has alluded: If it's not worth teaching, it's not worth testing. When teachers use complex tasks in which skills and concepts are first taught explicitly and then embedded in thoughtful applications, they build the assessment into the performance of the complex task. For example, while grammar instruction with direct attention to noun-verb agreement is necessary, the application of these grammatical rules in a written narrative is the "proof in the pudding." Thus, the instructional task becomes the assessment tool.

Teachers can achieve learning in this way by teaching for conceptual understanding and toward life skills that target what students need to know and be able to do—skills and concepts valued in the culture (Gardner 1983). Focusing on culturally valued skills puts the focus on learning for life, as well as preparing students for the test. One illustration of this type of teaching focus is in the realm of mathematics. If students conceptually understand the Pythagorean principles, then they know why houses are built with triangular supports. In turn, their depth of understanding serves them as they address this type of math problem on a test.

Teachers can also use "big" ideas to help students make thematic connections that foster deep understanding. For example, when teaching vocabulary, teachers can cluster words in meaningful groupings so the connectivity and association skills invoked by clustering facilitate the learning. Just as foreign language classes teach vocabulary in the form of thematic groupings such as the human body, foods, clothing, and travel, vocabulary development in reading, literature, science, and social studies can benefit from this umbrella approach as well.

Teachers can promote transfer and application of what they are teaching when they require the transfer through performance (Perkins and Salomon 1988). Teachers can incorporate Gardner's multiple intelligences theory (1983) as a way for students to express what they know. These intelligences fall into eight categories: verbal, visual, logical, musical, bodily, interpersonal, intrapersonal, and naturalist (see Figure 2). Teachers can explore the different intelligence areas with students, helping them create a bridge from what they already know to the new learning. It may also be helpful for teachers to ask questions that foster linkages: How does this connect to something you already know? How might you use this? Does the idea spark a connection to something you already use? (Noller, Parnes and Biondi 1976).

In an effort to prepare students for life's endeavors by providing them with solid skills and conceptual understandings, teachers also prepare students for the types of skills and concepts that appear on the tests they give. To teach *for* the test rather than *to* the test, serves the goals and main objectives of schooling—to educate young people for life.

Gardner's Multiple Intelligences

Visual/Spatial
Images, graphics, drawings, sketches, maps, charts, doodles, pictures, spatial orientation, puzzles, designs, looks, appeal, mind's eye, imagination, visualization, dreams, nightmares, films, and videos.

Logical/Mathematical
Reasoning, deductive and inductive logic, facts, data, information, spreadsheets, databases, sequencing, ranking, organizing, analyzing, proofs, conclusions, judging, evaluations, and assessments.

Verbal/Linguistic
Words, wordsmiths, speaking, writing, listening, reading, papers, essays, poems, plays, narratives, lyrics, spelling, grammar, foreign languages, memos, bulletins, newsletters, newspapers, E-mail, FAXes, speeches, talks, dialogues, and debates.

Musical/Rhythmic
Music, rhythm, beat, melody, tunes, allegro, pacing, timbre, tenor, soprano, opera, baritone, symphony, choir, chorus, madrigals, rap, rock, rhythm and blues, jazz, classical, folk, ads and jingles.

Bodily/Kinesthetic
Art, activity, action, experiental, hands-on, experiments, try, do, perform, play, drama, sports, throw, toss, catch, jump, twist, twirl, assemble, disassemble, form, re-form, manipulate, touch, feel, immerse, and participate.

Interpersonal/Social
Interact, communicate, converse, share, understand, empathize, sympathize, reach out, care, talk, whisper, laugh, cry, shudder, socialize, meet, greet, lead, follow, gangs, clubs, charisma, crowds, gatherings, and twosomes.

Intrapersonal/Introspective
Self, solitude, meditate, think, create, brood, reflect, envision, journal, self-assess, set goals, plot, plan, dream, write, fiction, nonfiction, poetry, affirmations, lyrics, songs, screenplays, commentaries, introspection, and inspection.

Naturalist
Nature, natural, environment, listen, watch, observe, classify, categorize, discern patterns, appreciate, hike, climb, fish, hunt, snorkle, dive, photograph, trees, leaves, animals, living things, flora, fauna, ecosystem, sky, grass, mountains, lakes, and rivers.

From *Problem-Based Learning and Other Curriculum Models for the Multiple Intelligences Classroom* by Robin Fogarty. © 1997 by IRI/SkyLight Training and Publishing, Inc. Reprinted with permission of SkyLight Professional Development, Arlington Heights, IL.

Figure 2

E   Expect the Best; Accept No Less

Teachers can foster lifelong learning by setting high expectations for all students. Teachers can accomplish this by giving students equal time and opportunity to respond to information. They can use wait time strategies to allow students time to think, to internalize their thoughts, and to make the necessary connections for a thoughtful response. Wait-time strategies involve pausing three to ten seconds following a teacher-generated question and then another three to six seconds following a student's response (Rowe 1987). Teachers can also use a systematic rotation to ensure they call on all students to respond while they move about the classroom to keep the proximity factor ever-changing. This keeps students on alert and more ready to interact and respond as they become the students nearest to the constantly moving teacher.

It is also important that teachers use grade level or developmentally appropriate materials in their teaching to foster students' reading and comprehension of the material. If students cannot read something, they cannot comprehend it.

For example, a teacher once attempted to read a friend's dissertation on chemical bonding. The author had specialized in this field as a researcher at Xerox, and the teacher wanted to honor her friend's work and agreed to read his study. After the first page, the teacher felt she was in over her head. She had no idea what she was reading, could not understand the subject, and achieved little real comprehension. It is the same way with student reading. Students need to be able to handle the reading if they are to construct knowledge and make meaning from it.

Another way teachers can enhance all learning is to teach skills explicitly, and then enhance the basic learning through enrichment and acceleration as needed by individual students. Not all students have the same learning needs. As students connect cognitively to information, their personal experience and background lay the groundwork for the related neural connections (Caine and Caine 1994). Thus, the various experiences students have had cause them to learn differently than their peers. Each learner is unique, and each responds differently to incoming data.

Although students may learn differently, when instruction is grounded in national, state, and local standards and clear benchmarks are stated, high expectations will prevail for all. Teachers can use the standards to shape curriculum and to frame learning for all students. When teachers follow these guidelines, they can expect the best and accept no less.

S Structure With Cooperative Learning

Cooperative learning structures are an important part of effective student learning. Teachers can use small group interactions to foster student-to-student dialogue. They can accomplish this by incorporating key elements of cooperative learning research (Johnson and Johnson 1986). Teachers can foster positive interdependence by having students engage in an activity that requires teamwork. This could be something such as a social studies project that jigsaws the work among three to four students (see Figure 3). Teachers can hold students individually accountable for the work they do in teams through quizzes, tests, and projects. In addition, teachers can have students reflect on the group work to build more skillful teams. Teachers can accomplish this when they ask groups to discuss what they did well and what they might do differently next time (Bellanca and Fogarty 1990). Finally, teachers can address the social skills of the group, taking advantage of all "teachable moments." If a group argues, teachers can discuss how people can learn to disagree with the idea, not with the person. This way, students use the group work to discuss communication and conflict resolution skills as well as skills in leadership and team building (Johnson and Johnson 1986).

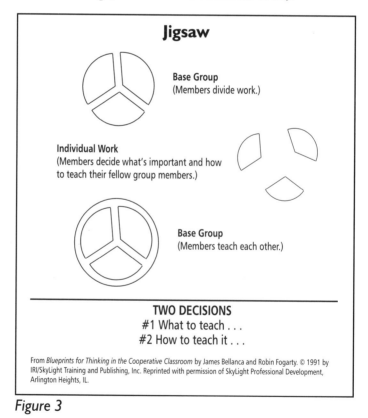

Jigsaw

Base Group
(Members divide work.)

Individual Work
(Members decide what's important and how to teach their fellow group members.)

Base Group
(Members teach each other.)

TWO DECISIONS
#1 What to teach . . .
#2 How to teach it . . .

From *Blueprints for Thinking in the Cooperative Classroom* by James Bellanca and Robin Fogarty. © 1991 by IRI/SkyLight Training and Publishing, Inc. Reprinted with permission of SkyLight Professional Development, Arlington Heights, IL.

Figure 3

Students need to work frequently in small groups to improve their ability to be part of a team effort. The number one reason people fail at their jobs is due to their inability to get along with their coworkers. The types of communication techniques practiced in group work are life skills that impact all human interactions—everything from the simple inferences that are drawn from facial expressions and body language to the sense of empathy that is felt for a friend or foe (Goleman 1995).

When teachers monitor small groups in cooperative learning structures they can "hear" what students are thinking and more easily facilitate their individual learning needs. In the course of group interactions, ideas are clarified and reflective thinking occurs. It's one thing when someone knows something, but it's quite another when he or she has to explain the ideas to someone else. When people discuss an idea, each captures the idea differently. In essence, thinking is crystallized as one struggles to relate his or her ideas to someone else so they both understand it in the same way. For example, teachers know the differences between inductive and deductive teaching, but it may be difficult for them to explain it to someone else. The task is the same for students in learning situations.

Cooperative learning can help students to better communicate and understand what they know. Research has found that cooperative learning is the number-one strategy for increased student achievement (Joyce 1986). When teachers structure their classroom instruction around using cooperative learning techniques they will see instant, visible, and positive differences in student work.

T Teach Test-Taking Strategies Explicitly

Teachers can help students prepare for test taking by demonstrating techniques for undertaking true/false, multiple choice, and essay questions. For example, some teachers teach their students techniques about what to do on an essay test when students have studied the wrong material. The advice teachers usually give is to make an over-arching statement and connect the response to the material students have studied. For example, "The concept of photosynthesis is much like the idea of the life cycle. They both ...." Chances are, this type of response will earn the student some points! Students can benefit from learning about these types of techniques to help them learn the best way to attack a question.

Additionally, teachers can counsel students to outline or web their ideas as soon as they read the test questions, "dumping" their ideas on paper and then revisiting and reconstructing them in a coherent essay. This quick reference web or outline takes the pressure off test-weary students and allows them to focus and proceed in a more systematic and organized way.

Teachers can teach test-taking strategies to help students become skillful at taking tests and at managing the different kinds of tests and test questions they will encounter throughout their lives. After all, if test taking is one of the gates students must pass through as they advance through the course called "schooling," why would teachers not provide practice to help them pass through that gate? Resources abound on the subject of skills for test taking. Books, articles, and programs specialize in preparation techniques for tests, and schools often provide courses in study skills and test-taking strategies, which are also helpful for students.

Teaching test-taking skills is a metacognitive strategy that empowers students. Teaching students to be able to plan, monitor, and evaluate their own test-taking abilities allows them to get better at taking tests. Once they become aware of their strengths and weaknesses regarding certain kinds of tests and responding to certain kinds of questions, they are better able to take control of their learning needs. The KWL strategy (Ogle 1986) helps students assess and plan for their learning needs (see Figure 4). This metacognitive realm of thinking about one's learning and one's thinking is at the heart of all learning (Brown 1980). Thus, teachers can let students in on the secrets and strategies of how to be good students and good test-takers by teaching test-taking strategies explicitly.

KWL		
K *What I Know*	**W** *What I Want to Know*	**L** *What I Have Learned*

Figure 4

S Stress Prelearning Strategies

Learners use what they already know to help them understand something new. One method teachers can use to assist student comprehension of new material is to stress prelearning strategies that tap into prior knowledge and past experiences. However, this technique is often contrary to common practice. In the past, reading lessons were focused as shown in Figure 5:

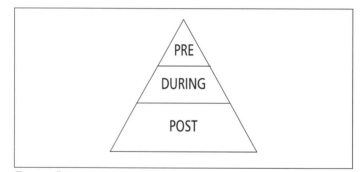

Figure 5

As exemplified by the triangular shape, teachers gave the least amount of attention to the prereading phase, asking a few questions about the title, characters, and pictures. Teachers gave a little more attention during the reading, posing monitoring questions as part of the round robin when doing oral reading. Teachers gave the most attention to the post-reading, or comprehension, questions. This is the model that many teachers are familiar with, because often this is the way they were taught.

However, research in the area of cognition and metacognition suggests that a more learner-friendly way to approach learning is through the inverted triangle model (see Figure 6).

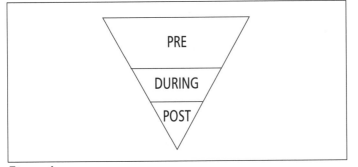

Figure 6

In this approach, teachers focus more time, energy, and discussion on the prereading or prelearning strategies (Anderson et al. 1985) to stimulate the background experiences and prior knowledge of the learners. If students are going to read about a dinner party, teachers can foster extensive student predictions about what kind of dinner party it might be, who (characters) might be at the party, where (setting) it will be, and what (plot) students anticipate might happen at the dinner party. After answering a question, students are prompted to justify why they are making that particular prediction. Once students have freely explored the possibilities based on their own experiences, they are primed for the reading. Their mindset is focused on the context, and they probably have covered certain vocabulary words in the predictions. When students enter the reading or learning situation with relaxed alertness (Caine and Caine 1994) toward the concepts, teachers have created a more brain-based approach for learning to occur (Wolfe 1996 and Sylwester 1995). When teachers stress prelearning strategies with their students, increased student achievement is the result.

C Chunk the Material for Deep Understanding

When studying new information, students sometimes find it hard to remember all the material, especially if it is complicated or elaborate. To help students remember long or complex sequences, teachers can cluster ideas together into chunks that make sense. It is important that teachers avoid teaching material only in discrete or isolated ways because doing so deters the connection-making process that is necessary for comprehension. As the brain sifts through incoming data, it acts like a sieve and filters out anything that does not get its attention. For ideas to be filtered into the memory system, ideas must have novelty, meaning, and relevance, or the brain will let go of them. Thus, the more "chunked" or connected an idea is, the more likely it will be noticed, manipulated, and anchored into the short- or long-term memory system (Wolfe 1996).

Consider students learning about different countries in a social studies class. If teachers cluster the information about Japan, South Africa, and the Netherlands around the ideas of government, economics, natural resources, and national customs, learners have these consistent chunks to consider as they compare and contrast the various cultures. Chunking is a way of remembering a series of facts or ideas as a single sequence or cluster.

Another method teachers can use to foster deep understanding, which fosters generalizations for transfer and application, is the technique of patterning ideas. For example, the concept of *systems* is understood by examining patterns of meaning about the *skeletal system*, the *computer system,* and the *postal system.* Teachers can create patterns as simple as the sequential patterns of beads on a string to as intricate as the patterns of geometric tessellations; as predictable as the patterns of sentence structure to as complex as patterns of poetry. Whatever pattern is revealed, memory is enhanced through the repetition and the wholeness demonstrated by the pattern.

Attaching meaning to a subject is the ultimate memory device. When something makes sense, it allows the learner to make the critical connection from previous understandings to new conceptualization, which results in learning. To learn means to have deep understanding and meaningful transfer of information. Teachers can cultivate such learning by chunking material and creating meaning through patterning for deep understanding.

0 Organize with Graphics

Just as cooperative learning groups make student thinking audible, graphic organizers make student thinking visible. When teachers ask students to represent their thinking graphically, students must organize the information and make sense of it to place it appropriately in the graphic. As students use a Venn diagram to contrast two characters from a novel, they must select the character attributes that are alike and those that are different to complete the graphic representation (see Figure 7).

By using a graphic organizer such as a Venn diagram, students can prepare their ideas for an essay by plotting out the similarities and differences of the characters prior to writing. When this is done, students are less likely to omit making comparisons and contrasts. If students bypass the graphic organizer, they might only

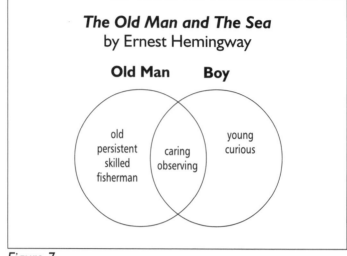

Figure 7

address one aspect of the characters. They might write about all the similarities or all the differences rather than both, which provides a fuller portrait of the two characters.

Graphic organizers or other theory-embedded tools such as concept maps, webs, flowcharts, and matrices offer visual organization to student thinking. Using graphic organizers taps into the visual/spatial intelligence (Gardner 1983), which gives students another way of learning, understanding, and expressing their ideas (Lyman and McTighe 1988).

Another critical component of the graphic organizer is in the realm of the metacognitive or reflective self. This pertains to being able to recognize *when* to use *what* to organize ideas. Teachers can help students practice this component by introducing students to a series of graphic organizers such as the fishbone, mind map, attribute web, and cause/effect circles. Then, students can select the best graphic organizers for the task teachers give them. For example, a sequence or flow-chart may be the best choice to use to plot a story, while cause/effect circles may work better for a science experiment. Eventually, students can create their own graphics to depict the information given to them.

One teacher relates the story of being asked to represent the mounds of information from her dissertation study through a graphic on a single sheet of paper. She was astounded that she was able to take that mountain of paper and reduce it to a lone graphic. In addition, she felt that the process clarified, crystallized, and enlightened what she learned from her work. It can be the same way with students. Graphic organizers can serve to educate them about what they have learned. Teachers can organize with graphics to increase student learning and student progress.

R Reflect Through Mediation

Reflective thinking is an important aspect of learning. One technique teachers can use to promote reflective thinking is human mediation. When using this technique, the teacher intervenes between the learner and the material, acting as the mediator of the learning (Feuerstein 1980). Teachers probe with questions, thus helping students link their thinking to the learning. Teachers foster reflective dialogue that helps students make sense of ideas and think strategically for the necessary transfer of learning into applicable situations. For example, as students struggle with a math problem, teachers can ask if they anticipate a larger number or a smaller one, and why. Teachers can then ask students to discuss a similar problem and what they did to solve that problem. In essence, teachers mediate the thinking process to help students unlock the keys to learning.

In addition, learning logs are reflective tools that teachers can use to encourage student thinking about the learning that just occurred. Through a stem or lead-in, teachers can lead students to think analytically (The hardest part was . . .), or decisively (The best part was . . .), or creatively (I wonder if . . .). Teachers can use learning logs prior to the learning to boot up reflections from the previous lesson, as monitoring techniques during the lesson ("Take a moment and jot down one idea before you go on."), or as an evaluation tool following the learning to assess understanding and quality of the work. The teacher mediation that is necessary when using learning logs is simply to employ them at appropriate times.

Students can sometimes mediate reflection as well. For example, think-aloud partner dialogues offer an optional mediation tool (Whimbey and Lockheed 1982). As two students work together as peer editors, they question each other on the meaning, the flow, and grammatical and structural usage of their writing. These reflective dialogues serve to educate students about their style of writing as they reflect on how they use written language.

Reflection is critical to learning, and teachers often inadvertently neglect it in the classroom because of the academic pressure to cover the content. Rapid-paced instruction is the result of that pressure, and in-depth dialogue and/or time for reflection become the casualties. Yet, research clearly demonstrates that reflection through metacognition is integral to increased student success. Consequently, teachers can reflect through mediation to achieve the results they want with student learning.

SkyLight Professional Development

Express Ideas With Mnemonic Devices and Visual Cues

Teachers can teach using memory devices to aid in learning, for learning and memory are inextricably linked (Wolfe 1996). First, an idea must capture the student's attention, and then it filters into short-term memory—if it has meaning and relevance. Finally, the idea may make it into long-term memory when it is used or associated with something else that is deeply internalized.

Mnemonic devices are very helpful in activating the metacognitive tools to enhance memory and learning. Many people remember the names of the Great Lakes by thinking of the acronym HOMES: Huron, Ontario, Michigan, Erie, and Superior. There's nothing like it. How about the acronym Touch Down, PFC? This one is harder—it's about the elements for effective training for teachers: theory, demonstration, practice, feedback, and coaching (Joyce and Showers 1983). Even though it may seem silly, it really works. The words Touch Down (T-D) go together naturally and PFC (Private First Call) is a combination of letters that is also familiar. Acronyms don't have to be logical—they just have to be memorable. Rhyming words and jingles can also help students remember things. "Yours is not to reason why, just invert and multiply" is a reminder about dividing fractions. The rhyme "I before E, except after C—except in neighbor and weigh," helps students remember how to spell receipt. These rhymes are fun to use and to develop with students as students become aware of strategies that enhance their memory and learning.

Visual cues are also helpful in trying to remember various facts, data, and information. The acronym ACE is a reminder of a visual cueing used by Lorayne and Lucas (1984). "A" stands for action, "C" is for color, and "E" signals exaggeration. Teachers can apply the concepts of action, color, and exaggeration to an idea to help students remember.

Visual cues also include the use of metaphors to recall information. This type of cue is shown in Walberg's metaphor of schooling (1984) in which he used the analogy of a three-legged stool. He made the point that three legs—parent, teacher, and child—are necessary for effective schooling. Just as a three-legged stool cannot stand without all three legs, neither can the school setting be functionally complete without all three of these components. Likewise, similes and metaphors are often used to teach: a president is like a king or justice is like a scale. These are tools that enhance memory and learning. Teachers can use tools such as these to express ideas with mnemonic devices and visual cues to effect increased student mastery over learning.

S Seek Student Choices in Learning Situations

To foster greater learning, teachers should allow students to have freedom of choice within a given learning structure. Teachers can set up the broad parameters while still allowing students to have some personal choices within that framework. In problem-based learning (PBL), after the problem has been defined, students direct the investigation according to the avenues that are revealed, student interest, and the natural flow of aligned curriculum (Stepien and Gallagher 1993 and Fogarty 1997). In other examples of PBL, students choose among three different novels about friendship, or students who are expected to read a biography and report on it through presentation, choose their "creative genius" from the fields of art, politics, sports, etc. In this way, students are making choices in their own learning.

If teachers capitalize on student interest and provide self-selection opportunities, students feel empowered about their own learning. This self-awareness of feelings is inextricably linked to their emotional intelligence and its impact on learning. Emotions are the gatekeeper to the intellect (Sylwester 1995). When students are emotionally hooked, the whole memory system is on alert—open to making sense and making meaning (Sylwester 1995)—and is searching for neural connections and pathways to long-term memory.

In another sense, when the learning is relevant, when students understand that multiplying fractions is not a mere exercise in the book, but that it is necessary for understanding recipes, pattern making, carpentry, music, etc., the learning takes on a deeper mission. Once this understanding occurs, learning is purposeful and meaningful. Everyone has experienced the motivating force that drives people to learn something because they need it to do something they want to do. Computer novices have learned to compute, keyboard, cut and paste text, and use Power Point because they needed to use these skills. That relevant need for the learning is the most powerful driving force for learners, and the performance is the built-in assessment (Stiggens 1991). When students are interested in knowing something, they are much more motivated to learn. It is in this way that teachers can use the technique of seeking student choices in learning situations to promote increased student achievement.

References

Anderson, Richard C., et al. 1985. *Becoming a nation of readers: The report of the Commission on Reading.* Washington, DC: National Institute of Education.

Anderson, T. H. 1980. Study strategies and adjunct aids. In *Theoretical issues in reading comprehension,* edited by R. J. Spiro, B. C. Bruce, and W. F. Brewer. Hillsdale, NJ: Erlbaum.

Bellanca, J., and R. Fogarty. 1990. *Catch them thinking: A handbook of classroom strategies.* Palatine, IL: Skylight Training and Publishing, Inc.

Brown, A. L. 1980. Metacognitive development and reading. In *Theoretical issues in reading comprehension,* edited by R. J. Spiro, B. C. Bruce, and W. F. Brewer. Hillsdale, NJ: Erlbaum.

Caine, Renate N., and Geoffrey Caine. 1994. *Making connections: Teaching and the human brain.* Reading, MA: Addison-Wesley.

Eisner, Elliot. 1983, October. The kinds of schools we need. *Educational Leadership:* 48–55.

Feuerstein, Reuven. 1980. *Instrumental Enrichment.* Baltimore, MD: Univeristy Park Press.

Fogarty, R. 1997. *Problem-based learning and other curriculum models for the multiple intelligences classroom.* Arlington Heights, IL: IRI/SkyLight Training and Publishing, Inc.

Gardner, Howard. 1983. *Frames of mind: The theory of multiple intelligences.* New York: Basic Books.

Goleman, Daniel. 1995. *Emotional intelligence.* New York: Bantam.

Johnson, R., and D. Johnson. 1986. *Circles of learning: Cooperation in the classroom.* Alexandria, VA: Association for Supervision and Curriculum Development.

Joyce, B. 1986. *Improving America's schools.* New York: Longman.

Joyce, B., and B. Showers. 1983. *Power in staff development through research and training.* Alexandria, VA: Association for Supervision and Curriculum Development.

Joyce, B., J. Wolf, and E. F. Calhoun. 1993. *The self-renewing school.* Alexandria, VA: Association for Supervision and Curriculum Development.

Kagan, Spencer. 1992. *Cooperative learning structures.* San Clemente, CA: Kagan Cooperative.

Kerman, Sam. 1979, June. Teacher expectations and student achievement. *Phi Delta Kappan* 60: 716–718.

Lorayne, Harry, and Jerry Lucas. 1974. *The memory book.* New York: Stein & Day.

McTighe, Jay, and Frank Lyman. 1988, April. Cueing thinking in the classroom: The promise of theory-embedded tools. *Educational Leadership* 45: 18–24.

Noller, R., S. Parnes, and A. Biondi. 1976. *Creative action book.* New York: Charles Scribner & Sons.

Ogle, Donna. 1986. K-W-L: A teaching model that develops active reading of expository text. *The Reading Teacher* 6: 564–570.

Perkins, David, and G. Salomon. 1988, September. Teaching for transfer. *Educational Leadership:* 22–32.

Rowe, Mary Budd. 1987, Spring. Wait time: Slowing down may be a way of speeding up. *Educator* 11(i): 43.

Stepien, W., and S. Gallagher. 1993, April. Problem-based learning: As authentic as it gets. *Educational Leadership:* 25–28.

Stiggens, R. 1991, March. Assessment literacy. *Phi Delta Kappan:* 534–539.

Sylwester, Robert. 1995. *A celebration of neurons: An educator's guide to the brain.* Alexandria, VA: Association for Supervision and Curriculum Development.

Walberg, H. L. 1984. Families as partners in educational productivity. *Phi Delta Kappan* 65 (6): 397–400.

Whimbey, A., and J. Lockheed. 1982. *Problem solving and comprehension.* Philadelphia: Franklin Institute Press.

Wolfe, Pat. 1996. *Live seminars on tape: Translating brain research into classroom practice* (3 audiotapes). Alexandria, VA: Association for Supervision and Curriculum Development.

There are
one-story intellects,
two-story intellects, and
three-story intellects with skylights.

All fact collectors, who have no aim beyond their
facts, are

one-story minds.

Two-story minds
compare, reason, generalize,
using the labors of the fact collectors
as well as their own.

Three-story minds
idealize, imagine, predict—their best illumination
comes from above,

through the **skylight**.

—Oliver Wendell Holmes

PROFESSIONAL DEVELOPMENT

We Prepare Your Teachers Today for the Classrooms of Tomorrow

Learn from Our Books and from Our Authors!

Ignite Learning in Your School or District.

SkyLight's team of classroom-experienced consultants can help you foster systemic change for increased student achievement.

Professional development is a process not an event. SkyLight's experienced practitioners drive the creation of our on-site professional development programs, graduate courses, research-based publications, interactive video courses, teacher-friendly training materials, and online resources—call SkyLight Professional Development today.

SkyLight specializes in three professional development areas.

Specialty # 1 Best Practices — We **model** the best practices that result in improved student performance and guided applications.

Specialty # 2 Making the Innovations Last — We help set up **support** systems that make innovations part of everyday practice in the long-term systemic improvement of your school or district.

Specialty # 3 How to Assess the Results — We prepare your school leaders to encourage and **assess** teacher growth, **measure** student achievement, and **evaluate** program success.

Contact the SkyLight team and begin a process toward long-term results.

2626 S. Clearbrook Dr., Arlington Heights, IL 60005
800-348-4474 • 847-290-6600 • FAX 847-290-6609
info@skylightedu.com • www.skylightedu.com